CW00685819

ISBN: 978129036869

Published by:
HardPress Publishing
8345 NW 66TH ST #2561
MIAMI FL 33166-2626

Email: info@hardpress.net
Web: http://www.hardpress.net

Sligo

Lough Gill   Glencar
Rosses Point   Inishmurray
and Surroundings

For fuller information, see the Company's New
Illustrated Guide Book (Price 6d.)

FOREWORD

Modern travelling facilities have placed the WEST OF IRELAND within easy reach of all parts of the United Kingdom, and there is no longer any reason why this magnificently endowed district of the Homelands should not become one of the most favoured of all our Holiday Resorts.

BRITISH VISITORS coming to Ireland have the choice of many ways; but for SLIGO and the West the DIRECT ROUTE is to Holyhead on the London and North Western System, and thence by fast steamer to Dublin.

The Channel-crossing may be made either by the "Irish Mail" or the "Irish Express," and is reduced to a minimum by the great efficiency and rapidity of the large and splendidly-equipped passenger fleets on these specialised services.

A three hours' sea trip brings the visitor to Dublin, a handsome city entered through a beautiful Bay; and thence the way to the West —a matter of four or five hours—is direct by the Midland Great Western Railway, starting from the Broadstone Station.

This journey is rendered pleasant by the up-to-date comforts and catering provided, and by the varied charms of many of the scenes traversed, which offer, as it were, a foretaste of the richer glories at its end.

SLIGO

CLIMAX TO THE IRISH GRAND TOUR— LOUGH GILL — BOATING, DRIVING, MOTORING — ROSSES POINT AND STRANDHILL — SPLENDID GOLFING AND FISHING

THE West of Ireland is a country of peerless attractions for the holiday-seeker and the sportsman. Happily in these days the extent and variety of its extraordinary advantages are so well known that the British tourist is almost wilfully closing his eyes to the light if he continues to ignore the wonderful scenes of natural beauty and of healthful, bracing enjoyment that lie so close within his reach. That class of tourist is diminishing rapidly, and surely the enterprising public to whom this little book is addressed will not be content to be numbered among an expiring type.

OPPORTUNITY NOT TO BE MISSED.

Clearly, you *must* come to our Western Highlands and Seaboards some time or other ; else your reputation as a connoisseur, as a traveller of intelligence, will be sadly dimmed. And if this be so, why postpone an experience which can be nothing short of delightful when it comes ? Summers succeed one another and are numbered with the past ; life slips by ; opportunities occur, but do not often repeat themselves. Look at the matter philosophically, therefore, and decide that the claims of the Irish Grand Tour of the West are irresistible this season.

MANIFOLD ATTRACTIONS.

Every part of the West of Ireland is conveniently reached by the Midland Great Western Railway from Dublin, and the Company have done a great deal within recent years to open up this glorious land in the most modern fashion for the comfort of visitors. Railway extensions have been made, and excellent services put on the lines; fine hotels have been erected on romantic lakesides amidst the sheltering hills; golf courses have been laid down, fishing waters rented and preserved—for our West is an angler's paradise, and its abundant loughs and streams are agleam with the speckle of fine salmon and trout; motor coaches have been set running on the highways, to link up the various railway branches and to provide visitors with luxurious road travelling in these most invigorating districts.

OUR PURPOSE.

In the Handbook to the West of Ireland, published by the Railway Company, will be found full particulars of these inspiring tours and their accessory pleasures; and in a series of companions to the present little book some of the chief centres—GALWAY, CONNEMARA, WESTPORT and ACHILL, etc.—are specially dealt with in a handy form for easy reference. We here purpose to do a similar service for SLIGO, which is the headquarters of another great division of the famed West of Ireland Tour.

SLIGO.

ROMAN CATHOLIC CATHEDRAL, SLIGO.

Photo by] [*Laurence, Dublin.*

MARKET STREET, SLIGO.

Photo by] [*Laurence, Dublin.*

BOAT HARBOUR, RIVERSIDE, SLIGO.

A LITERARY TRIBUTE.

In endeavouring to recommend this district to the attention of visitors from beyond our seas, we can adopt no better or truer text than the appreciation which follows from the pen of an eminent literary authority, the late Mr. Alfred Austin, Poet Laureate. He was an ardent lover of Irish natural beauty, as his books amply show, and among all his wanderings, the leisurely summers which he gave to our Western hills and seaboards appear to have filled him with the sincerest and most enthusiastic admiration. Happily there are many British and foreign visitors of discernment such as he. We quote, therefore, as very apt to our purpose an eloquent passage from Mr. Austin's *Spring and Autumn in Ireland*, noting that what he says on the subject of Connaught generally will apply in full measure to that portion of it included in the Sligo Tours.

FOR THE ARTIST.

" Why," asks the poet, " do not English artists take their easels, their sketch-books, and their umbrella tents to Ireland ? I have heard some of them complain that though English scenery may be very ' nice ' and amply supply matter for the poet, it is too unpicturesque for the painter, who must perforce cross the Alps in search of what he needs. Then, let the picturesque-hunting artist go to Ireland, to Connemara, to Mayo, to Donegal, to Sligo, and he will find endless variety of form and attitude in the lofty and circular hills. If he be in search of colour, I think he ought to make Ireland his home."

Nature's Colouring.

" The writer is fairly familiar with Italy," Mr. Austin proceeds, " and Greece and the Aegean are not unknown to him. He once passed a month at Perugia, gazing at the lights and shadows in heaven and on earth, on the mountains, in sky, on the plain which the great Umbrian painters have tried to reproduce in the background of their altarpieces. But the colouring on mountain gorge, mountain slope, and mountain gully, on lake shore and lake island, on wood and plain and bog, in Ireland, in intermittent hours of sunshine, would have shown even Raphael something more, and imbued the landscape in Perugino's frescoes with yet more tenderness.

" Iridescent Loveliness."

" It is as though all the rainbow hues of Nature, that fail to find in the uniform sea and sky of the wide Atlantic, a fitting and sufficiently sensitive canvas, discharged their iridescent loveliness on the mountain brows and ocean fronts. . . . There Nature works her own colours on her own palette with her own dew—the moisture of the atmosphere renders the task so easy. Often, no doubt, she seems dissatisfied with her work, blurs all the picture with mist, or even, as it were, effaces it with discontented hand. But that is only in order to perfect her conception on the morrow."

It was this wonderful property of our Western scenes, together with the mixture of humour and romance which he found among its people, that

Photo by]   *[Lawrence, Dublin.*

HAZELWOOD, LOUGH GILL, CO. SLIGO.

Photo by]   *[Lawrence, Dublin.*

LOUGH GILL, CO. SLIGO.

Photo by]   [Lawrence, Dublin.

GLENCAR, CO. SLIGO.

Photo by]   [Lawrence, Dublin.

GLENCAR LAKE, CO. SLIGO.

moved the gentle poet to his parting exhortation : " Go to Ireland, and go often. It is a delightful country to travel in."

Sligo's Claims.

It is true that many travellers reserve Sligo as a grand finale to a holiday in Connemara or in other districts already named ; and no better arrangement can be made by people of abundant leisure who are prepared to give Sligo its due. But Sligo is self-contained ; it can itself be selected as a charming place for a considerable stay, as well as being included in a general western holiday. You may combine it with Connemara and Westport, reaching it at length through Ballina ; or starting direct from the Broadstone Station, Dublin, you may make Sligo and its vicinity the independent object of your itinerary. And in any case, it is hoped that the following suggestions will not be without interest to either class of visitors.

Good Town and Comfortable Quarters.

With its population of 11,163, according to the last census, Sligo is a good prosperous looking country town, which provides excellent quarters for visitors. The *Victoria Hotel*, in Albert Street, may justly claim to be one of the best in Ireland. Other commodious houses are the *Imperial*, overlooking the river close to Upper (or New) Bridge, and *Ramsay's Temperance Hotel*, also overlooking the river on the north side of the Upper Bridge.

Of Public Buildings, there are none requiring

detailed description; the most noteworthy is the *Roman Catholic Cathedral*. The building opposite the Victoria Hotel is the *Court-House*. The new *Post Office* is in Knox Street, with sub-office in Castle Street.

An Ancient Abbey.

Within the town is an object which will appeal to people with antiquarian interests. This is Sligo Abbey, adjoining Abbey Street. It was founded for Dominicans, in 1252, by Maurice Fitzgerald, Lord of Offaly, who was grandson of one of the Anglo-Norman invaders, Maurice Fitzgerald. He also founded the Franciscan houses of Youghal (1224) and Ardfert (1253). In 1414, Sligo Abbey was greatly injured by an accidental fire, but was almost immediately restored, and it is to this fifteenth-century work that most of the existing ruins belongs. The portion of interest are the church and cloisters. What is left of domestic buildings is mere shapeless masonry.

The Remains.

The nave of the church retains three arches of its arcade on the south side, and two windows on the north side where also is an elaborate Crane tomb, 1616. The small central tower is noticeable for its vaulting and the corbels of its west arch. The choir preserves five lancet windows of the earlier building, but the east window belongs to the rebuilding. It is decorated and of four lights. The high altar, in nine compartments, has an incised cross on its slab. The carved stone, a figure with three hearts upon it, is the crest of the O'Conor, who is commemorated by the mural monuments, 1623.

The cloisters are practically entire on three sides, and are of the small type common in Irish monasteries. They have long been converted from an ambulatory into a burial-place, so that the dimensions appear yet smaller than they structurally are. Interments within the Abbey have only recently ceased.

EXCURSIONS FROM SLIGO.

Lough Gill.

Within easy reach of Sligo is Lough Gill— "the Killarney of the West"—a natural feature of the district, which in itself is enough to lend it a distinction of the highest order. This exquisitely beautiful lake—some 5 miles long and from 1 to 1½ broad has few rivals in the British Isles. The richly wooded shores, perfect islets, and the environment of shapely hills, are its distinctive features. It can be viewed in various ways—on foot, by boat, and by carriage.

(*a*) On Foot or Driving.—Leave the town by the road that continues Albert Street southward, and beyond the cemetery go to the left. In a mile more, that is two miles from the hotels, a charming view is obtained. In returning it would be well to diverge, right, to *Cairns Hill*, so called from the mound which crowns it. The prospect thence is as comprehensive as it is beautiful, and includes Sligo, always a pleasant object from its environs, Lough Gill, and the cliffs of the Benbulbin range.

(*b*) BY BOAT.—About 5 miles south from Upper (or New) Bridge. The River Garvogue, which drains Lough Gill, widens a short distance above the town, and descends through the delightful demesne of HAZELWOOD—visitors admitted to the grounds—of which the mansion is on the peninsular north bank at the entrance to the lake. A short distance up the lake near the south shore is *Cottage Island*. Half-way up the lake is *Church Island*, the largest in the lake. It gets its name from having been in early times a monastic retreat. Some slight remains are extant, and the burial ground is still, we believe, used.

(*c*) DRIVE ROUND THE LAKE.—About 24 miles, for 12*s.*, passing about half-way through Dromahair, where the ruins of *Crevelea Abbey*, a sixteenth-century Franciscan monastery, can be visited.

A DELIGHTFUL OUTING.

The drive is undoubtedly the most satisfactory way of seeing Lough Gill, and Cairns Hill, already mentioned, can be included by a trifling detour. After a lovely bit alongside the lake, the road ascends a charming glen, and then turns eastward to Dromahair. Thence, in about a mile and a-half, east, it returns to the lake, and skirts its end past Newtown Castle. Along the north side, the *old* road, which, for some two miles, is between the lake and the *new* road, is rough but practicable, and should certainly be preferred. A fleet of well-equipped motor boats ply daily, from

Photo by]   *[Lawrence, Dublin.*
CROSS AT DRUMCLIFF, CO. SLIGO.

CLUBHOUSE, COUNTY SLIGO GOLF CLUB, ROSSES POINT.

Photo by] *[Lawrence, Dublin.*
ROSSES POINT, CO. SLIGO.

Photo by] *[Lawrence, Dublin.*
NEW ROAD, STRANDHILL, CO. SLIGO.

May to October, between the riverside at Sligo and the pier at Dromahair.

FISHING.

Lough Gill is a good water for salmon, white trout, brown trout, and pike. Fly and spinning, especially eel-tail, are the lures. " The salmon run small, but as their passage from the sea is short, they are killed in full dress of marine parade." Permits for free fishing can be obtained at the Hotels already named.

KNOCKNAREA AND CARROWMORE.

The former of these is the isolated limestone hill (1,078 feet) between Sligo Bay and Bally-sodare Bay ; the latter is a collection of 60 or 70 Celtic antiquities—cairns, stone circles, etc.—said to represent the graves of the slain in the battle of Moytura. The drive round Knocknarea is about 12 miles, and to include Carrowmore (which is to the south of it) would add about 2 miles. Most tourists will find their account in visiting the GLEN ; and then ascending the hill, and descending to Strandhill on the N.W. side, where there are several small, but comfortable Hotels.

PICTURESQUE GLEN.

We leave the town by Church Street, pass under the railway, and keep straight on for about 5½ miles to Knocknaheer. The Glen is between this road and the lower road, and is a deep and narrow cleft in the limestone, about half-a-mile long, charmingly set off by greenery, all the more gracious because of the sterility of the hill.

A Great Cairn.

From the summit of Knocknarea, which is occupied by a huge cairn (reputed to mark the burial-place of Maev, the legendary Queen of Connaught at the beginning of the Christian era), the view is a genuine reward for the ascent : north lies Donegal Bay, with Slieve League unmistakable ; nearer to the right are the cliffs of the Benbulbin range ; east is Sligo, very picturesque from here, and beyond is sylvan Lough Gill ; south-west the cone of Nephin may be detected 40 miles away ; west, it is Downpatrick Head that bounds the coast view. The descent to Strandhill from the plateau passes to the left of two caves, and then becomes a path bearing to the right. After that the way is down fields into the village, or to the road a little east of it.

Glencar.

The fine drive round this lough is 20 miles out and home. The WATERFALLS, three in number, are about twelve minutes apart, in a glen on the north side, near the east end of the lough, and at Glencar Cottage refreshments and a guide can be obtained. The three falls are very distinct. The *lowest* is a sheer fall of 40 feet ; the *middle* is smaller but higher, though more of a cascade ; *the uppermost* and highest can only be viewed from above. It is, perhaps, the most impressive as it rushes down into a veritable abyss, which is inaccessible. If the traveller merely drives to Glencar Cottage, the distance from Sligo will be about 7½ miles.

THE GLEN, STRANDHILL, CO. SLIGO.

TEELING MONUMENT, CARRIGNAGAT, CO. SLIGO.

[Lawrence, Dublin.
BALLYSODARE FALLS, CO. SLIGO.

[Lawrence, Dublin.
MARKREE CASTLE. SLIGO.

ROSSES POINT.

A Superb Seaside Resort.

No sojourn in this district—however brief—could be satisfactory, if it did not include a visit to Rosses Point, and, if possible, one should arrange to spend at least a few days there. The beauty of the place is superb, and local enterprise is now supplementing the natural attractions by many amenities that will appeal strongly to the stranger. Rosses Point is within five miles of Sligo Station, and can be reached either by car or by motor boat.

Splendid Golf Course.

Among its many inducements to extended patronage is the fact that it possesses an improved eighteen-holes golf course, which is justly regarded as one of the finest in Ireland. The Club that maintains it has spared no pains to render this fine sea course as perfect as it is possible to make any links. Several new bunkers have been recently made ; the course has been greatly improved, and is bound to increase every year in popularity. A new and commodious club house has lately been erected at considerable cost. The Golf Links Hotel is most pleasantly situated, and is under courteous and efficient management. In addition, there are several small, but acceptable places of accommodation in the village.

One of the charms of Rosses Point is " grand golf at small expense "—visitors' fees, Gentlemen 2s. per day, 10s. per week ; Ladies 1s. 6d. per day, 7s. 6d. per week; Sunday play allowed with caddies. The Club is affiliated to the Golfing Union of Ireland.

MOUNTAIN AND SEA.

" On arrival at Rosses Point," says a recent writer, " and more especially on the course, one is first almost overcome by the magnificent views of sea and mountains. To the north is the pretty estate of Sir Josslyn Gore Booth; while close to it is the mountain of Benbulbin. Away to the south-west stretch the Mayo coast and mountains, and nearer Sligo are Lissadell, Knocknarea, etc. On clear days the Donegal Mountains show up well beyond Bundoran. Having got over the views, the visitor next becomes aware of the strength and invigorating freshness of the air, which is Rosses Point's most favourable asset. So many seaside places become relaxing in Summer; but three rounds of 18 holes on the Co. Sligo course scarcely tire one, a fact due to the air and the very pleasant walking. A strong point of the Sligo Club is the very warm welcome extended to visitors, who need never be afraid of being left out in the cold, even if they do not know any resident."

IMPORTANT UNDERTAKING.

It should be mentioned that the Midland Great Western Railway Company purpose building at Rosses Point a new hotel on the most modern lines, and hope to have it opened for visitors early in 1915. This undertaking will do much to enhance the special advantages which the

locality already enjoys, and will ensure that
every visitor shall be most comfortably looked
after. Rosses Point is indeed fortunate in the
recognition which it has won for itself.

During the summer months public cars ply
daily between Rosses Point and Sligo.

STRANDHILL.

ANOTHER BEAUTY OF THE BAY.

Facing Rosses Point, on the other side of the
Bay, is Strandhill, a rising seaside resort, four
miles from Sligo. It, too, is a place that must
be seen by every conscientious visitor to these
parts. It is situated at the foot of Knocknarea,
is adjacent to a most picturesque glen, and has
a magnificent level strand, over two miles long,
and very safe for bathing. The sea bathing is
perfect, and in addition, well equipped hot
and cold Salt Water Baths, with tea-rooms
attached, have recently been erected on the shore.

PROVISION FOR VISITORS.

Excellent accommodation is available at the
" Ocean View," " Atlantic," and " Star " Hotels,
and also at several boarding establishments.
The famous Culleenamore Oyster beds (now
worked by the Connacht Fisheries and Produce
Company) are in the vicinity. There is an ample
car service during the season between the Railway
Station and Strandhill.

BALLYSODARE.

On the line between Sligo and Collooney, is
Ballysodare, another little place which is showing

special signs of advancement. An important new flour milling industry has lately been started there by the firm of Messrs. Pollexfen & Co.

INISHMURRAY.

A Lonely Island in the Atlantic.

There is no regular communication with this island (1½ by ½ mile), which lies out in the Atlantic to the north of Sligo Bay. The distance from Sligo is about 20 miles, and only antiquaries will undertake the voyage for which they must charter their craft. " The group of ruins there," says Lord Dunraven, " offers the most characteristic example now in existence of the earliest monastic establishments in Ireland." These ruins, which comprise small churches or oratories, beehive huts, altars, etc., are chiefly within a great Stone Fort or Cashel, of Pagan origin.

The Inhabitants.

The repairing and refurbishing which the antiquities underwent some years ago, when they passed into the charge of the Board of Works, has robbed them somewhat of their venerable appearance. The people of the island are scarcely less interesting than the antiquities. They number somewhat over a hundred, and are said to be living in comparative comfort. Their chief food is barley, potatoes and fish, but each family has a cow or two, and a horse or donkey. The dress is of native homespun.

Lightning Source UK Ltd.
Milton Keynes UK
UKHW02f1125300718
326492UK00012B/771/P